Altered Board Book

BASICS & BEYOND

FOR CREATIVE SCRAPBOOKS, ALTERED BOOKS & ARTFUL JOURNALS

Jan Bode Smiley

C&T PUBLISHING

Text © 2005 Jan Bode Smiley, Artwork © C&T Publishing
Publisher: Amy Marson
Editorial Director: Gailen Runge
Acquisitions Editor: Jan Grigsby
Editor: Jan Grigsby
Copyeditor/Proofreader: Wordfirm Inc.
Cover Designer: Christina D. Jarumay
Design Director/Book Designer: Christina D. Jarumay
Production Assistant: Kerry Graham
Photography: Luke Mulks
Published by C&T Publishing, Inc., P.O. Box 1456, Lafayette, CA 94549

Front cover: *My Backyard Field Guide* Jan Bode Smiley

Attention Teachers: C&T Publishing, Inc., encourages you to use this book as a text for teaching. Contact us at 800-284-1114 or www.ctpub.com for more information about the C&T Teachers Program.

We take great care to ensure that the information included in this book is accurate and presented in good faith, but no warranty is provided nor results guaranteed. Having no control over the choices of materials or procedures used, neither the author nor C&T Publishing, Inc., shall have any liability to any person or entity with respect to any loss or damage caused directly or indirectly by the information contained in this book. For your convenience, we post an up-to-date listing of corrections on our web page (www.ctpub.com). If a correction is not already noted, please contact our Customer Service Department at ctinfo@ctpub.com or at P.O. Box 1456, Lafayette, CA 94549.

Trademarked (™) and Registered Trademark (®) names are used throughout this book. Rather than use the symbols with every occurrence of a trademark and registered trademark name, we are using the names only in the editorial fashion and to the benefit of the owner, with no intention of infringement.

Library of Congress Cataloging-in-Publication Data

Smiley, Jan Bode,
  Altered board book basics and beyond : for creative scrapbooks, altered
  books & artful journals / Jan Bode Smiley.
    p. cm.
  Includes index.
  ISBN 1-57120-309-5 (paper trade)
  1. Altered books. 2. Scrapbooks. I. Title.

  TT896.3.S52 2005
  702'.8'1--dc22

                        2004022886

Printed in Singapore 10 9 8 7 6 5 4 3 2 1

DEDICATION

To Tom –
thanks for being my rock, steady and strong.

To Emma and To Keith –
the best kids a Mom could hope for.

ACKNOWLEDGMENTS

Thanks to the C & T team for their incredible support. They are a truly amazing group.

I continue to shake my head in awe at the incredibly talented artists who produced wonderful new work for inclusion in this book. I thank them for their commitment when working under such a tight deadline.

I would like to thank the growing number of people who join me in exploring the "cross over" potential of other mediums. This is an exciting time for any quilter, book artist, painter, stamper, scrapbook artist or crafter as we discover just how much we have in common. I look forward to the day when we've erased all the lines, instead of just crossing over them. Until then, let's see how much fun we can have coloring outside the lines!

TABLE OF CONTENTS

INTRODUCTION

Why Altered Books?

People will ask you—trust me they will—"Why are you doing that to a book?" I have several standard answers for this question. One is simply "Because I can." A more interesting response is to ask them the question: "Why not?"

The process of altering books allows you to bring your unique collection of past experiences together, and it requires you to leave nothing behind as you start or continue on this altered path. If you have done embroidery or cross-stitch in your past, you can use your embroidery floss and stitching in your altered books. If you have done metal work or jewelry making, you might be anxious to add metal embellishments and wire work in your altered books. If you are a quiltmaker, you'll like the layering potential in your altered books. If you have painting experience, you'll be comfortable painting in your altered books. If you are a seamstress, you'll enjoy working with fabric, buttons, and closures in altered books. If you love to draw, altered books will give you unique surfaces on which to draw. If you have limited art or craft experience, altered books will invite you to explore as many or as few different mediums as you'd like. There are no "have tos" or "don't dos" in the altered book format, so *you* decide which techniques and materials to explore along *your* altered path.

The intimate nature of books, the fact that they are most easily viewed while being held, is a very personal act. Gently turning the pages in order to discover what awaits you on the next page; looking at each page again and again while discovering details you didn't see the first, second, or even third time you looked at the same page; starting back at the beginning as soon as you reach the end; the familiar form of books; the potential to create related work on each spread and to produce a cohesive body of work related to a theme or a series to be held in your hands—these are just some of the reasons I love altering books.

Why Alter Board Books?

A board book is a great place to start if you are at all nervous about pursuing altered book art. Altering board books, rather than paper books, offers several unique opportunities. First and foremost is the extra strength of the pages in board books. This enables you to incorporate heavier items without worrying about whether the page can support the added weight. Second, the limited number of spreads in most board books is a factor that I consider an asset. Third, you can complete an altered board book in a very reasonable amount of time; there is no worry about "working in this book forever before I finish." Fourth, completed altered board books display very nicely. The strength of the cover and pages allows them to stand up when they are finished.

Last but not least, altered board books offer endless prospects for great gifts. Within a short amount of time, you can easily create a one-of-a-kind altered book for any occasion. If you enjoy scrapbooking, board books will allow you to bring a new look to your scrapbook art. A special event or person can be honored in his or her own special book.

Altering BOARD **BOOKS**

Board books are wonderful bases for altered book projects. These books, generally thought of as children's books, are easy to find at reasonable prices, possibly even free from a friend whose children have outgrown them. The limited number of pages in most board books creates an accessible form: It's easier to get started when you know you won't be working forever before the artwork is complete.

If you are already familiar with altered books, board books afford wonderful opportunities to experiment with extra embellishments and mixed media endeavors. If you are a seasoned altered book artist, take advantage of the additional weight of the pages in board books, and challenge yourself with the added flexibility of this book form.

Whether you enjoy paint, special paper, fabric, stamping, or a combination of any and all of these techniques, altered board books enable you to express yourself through your art.

Before You Start to Alter
The quickest way to get started on an altered board book is to buy a blank board book made expressly for this purpose (see Resources on page 47 for information). These books are ready for you to begin your creative process *immediately*.

If you want to use a board book you already own, there are a few things you need to do before you start to alter it. Board books typically have a durable coating to help them survive hard use by children.

If you were to start altering right away, it would be easy to become frustrated: Paint and adhesives don't typically bond with slick surfaces. Following are three different methods of preparing traditional board book surfaces. Different books will require different approaches, and you may need to combine these techniques to successfully "prep" your board book.

Peeling
Start at a corner of a page and try peeling off the slick coating. If you're lucky, the top layer will peel off easily. Typically the book's artwork will peel off along with the glossy coating, leaving you with completely blank book pages ready for altering.

Peeling off the coated surface

Sanding
If the glossy surface of your board book does not separate and peel away from the base layer, try using sandpaper to prep the pages. This technique is best done outside; it *is* messy. Sand the shiny finish and artwork off the page.

Sanding the surface

If the page still feels slick after sanding, continue on to the next technique.

Applying Gesso
Not all board books have a thick, shiny top layer. Some books are made with a thinner board stock; in this case, you might not want to create a thinner base by peeling or sanding off layers. Perhaps all you need to do is apply gesso (see page 8 for information on gesso) to the pages before altering them. In this case, just coat the pages with gesso and allow each page to dry before proceeding.

I like to use foam brushes for applying gesso. Two layers—a thin layer brushed in one direction and dried, followed by another thin layer brushed in a perpendicular direction—will result in better coverage than one heavy application.

Your objective with any of these processes is the same: to adequately prepare the pages of your board book. The pages need to be ready to accept any paint, paper, ink, adhesive, fabric, or other materials that you choose to use when altering your book.

All of the instructional information throughout the remainder of this book assumes that you have completely prepped your pages or that you are using a blank board book.

Now that you've successfully prepped your book pages, let's get on with the more enjoyable aspects of book altering.

If you were impatient with these processes, purchase a Ready-to-Go blank board book to use next time.

Glossary OF MATERIALS

Acknowledging that everyone has different art and craft experiences in his or her background, this reference section explains terms and materials that you haven't had a chance to learn about yet. Rather than be intimidated by art supply, scrapbook, or quilt shops, read through this glossary of terms to become familiar with available products before you go shopping for supplies.

Acrylic Paint

Acrylic paints are wonderful to use in altered board books. They dry quickly, are readily available, and safe to use. You get what you pay for when purchasing acrylic paints. Inexpensive paint will have more "binder" and less pigment than pricier brands. My favorite brands are Jo Sonya's® and Golden®. My advice is to buy the best-quality paint you can afford.

GLAZING MEDIUM

Glazing medium is an acrylic medium that can be added to your acrylic paints to extend coverage and slow the drying time. If you want to extend the coverage you get from your high-quality acrylic paints, simply mix your paint with glazing medium. If you are an impatient person, you might want to think twice before adding this medium to your paint because it does slow the drying time. This slower drying time is a wonderful thing if you want to add texture to your page or if you are mixing colors as you work on your book pages.

Adhesives

There are many adhesives that can be used successfully in altered books. Following is a basic guide to adhesives and their most appropriate uses. As you work in the book format, you'll decide which one(s) you most like to use.

CRAFTER'S PICK ADHESIVES

The Ultimate, Fabric Glue, and Memory Mount are all Crafter's Pick brand glues. There are many more in this company's line, but these are my all-around favorite white glues. These thick, white glues are nontoxic, water-based adhesives that dry clear. Fabric Glue is specifically formulated for fabric and is washable. The Ultimate is great for adhering heavier items in your books. Memory Mount is acid-free. All of these dry fairly quickly and are very versatile.

DOUBLE STICK TAPE

For lightweight paper items, double stick tape is handy. Choose acid-free tape if that is important to you.

GEL MEDIUM

Gel medium is an acrylic polymer that can be added to acrylic paint to extend coverage. It can also be used as an adhesive. Gel medium is available in a variety of weights and finishes; compare and buy the one that *you* like best. Lightweight gel mediums are great for adhering paper and light fabric. Heavy gel mediums are good for adhering heavier and bulkier items.

GLUE STICKS

Some glue sticks create permanent bonds, some create temporary bonds, some are acid-free, some are colored so you can see where you've applied it on the page. Glue sticks are fast drying and easy to use. My favorite brand of glue stick is Uhu®, which is an acid-free product that is terrific for adhering small or lightweight items in books.

GOOD OLD WHITE GLUE

Close your eyes, remember the smell of white school glue, and you'll be transported back in time. Sometimes referred to as PVA, which stands for polyvinyl acetate, these water-based, synthetic adhesives are easy-to-use, multipurpose glues. Some are acid-free, so look for those if that is important to you. Although the labeling and consistency of glues may vary, they all share the same basic properties and should work well in your book projects.

SPRAY ADHESIVES

Many types of spray adhesives are available. One thing they all have in common is the need to use them outside so you don't breathe the fumes. Spray adhesives are convenient to use if you are in a hurry, but may not be the best choice if you are concerned about the long-term effects of the chemicals in the adhesive. Most spray adhesives are very strong, so be sure you place the item exactly where you want it because repositioning is difficult, if not impossible.

XYRON®

Xyron a brand machines apply dry adhesive to the back of flat items. The machines require no electricity and no batteries. Available in widths ranging from 5¹/₂" to 12", they can be found in most craft stores.

Xyron adhesive system

The advantages of applying dry adhesive with this product are that it doesn't distort paper and you don't have to wait for your adhesive to dry. Xyron systems are not inexpensive, so be sure you will use it enough to make the purchase worthwhile.

STILL STUCK ON ADHESIVES?

Refer to **www.thistothat. com** for more information on adhesives and the appropriate time to use them.

Brushes

Brushes are used to apply paint, gesso, ink, adhesive, and watercolor when working on altered books. My preference is to use inexpensive brushes. I like the disposable foam brushes for most applications. I use them a few times, rinse them out if possible, and throw them away when they get stiff.

Copyright

Copyright issues are important to consider in any medium. In the simplest of terms, it is not OK to make an altered book spread from images of other people's artwork and call it your own. I am not a legal expert, but I encourage you to learn about how copyright issues affect *your* artwork. **www.funnystrange.com/copy right/** is a terrific place to start when seeking information on copyright issues and collage.

Craft Knife

A craft knife, sometimes referred to as an X-Acto knife, has a very sharp blade. It can be used to cut paper, cardboard, plastic, and a variety of other materials. Always be careful when using this sharp tool, and remember that a sharp blade is safer to use than a dull one.

Craft knives

Decorative Edges Cutting Tools

Although tearing paper and fabric can be very satisfying, there are times when a special decorative edge might enhance your work. Several companies make scissors and rotary cutting blades with decorative patterns. Sharp rotary cutting blades that are intended for paper use can be used successfully on fabric also.

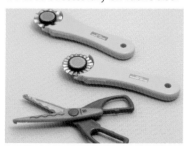
Decorative edge cutting tools

Ephemera (i-FEH-mer-ah)

According to *Merriam-Webster's Collegiate Dictionary*, ephemera is (1) something of no lasting significance, and (2) paper items (as posters, broadsides, and tickets) that were originally meant to be discarded after use but have since become collectibles.

According to collage artists, ephemera is probably what makes your artwork uniquely yours. Each of us has different "stuff" in our lives, and using those "insignificant" pieces of paper and memorabilia are what make your artwork unique. Examples of ephemera include ticket stubs, shopping receipts, clothing tags, postage stamps, handwritten notes, report cards, invitations, candy wrappers, maps, travel brochures, and so on.

Eyelets and Eyelet Setting Tools, including screw punchs

Eyelets come in countless sizes, colors, and shapes. They are available at fabric, scrapbook, and craft stores. Proper tools are essential to the successful use of eyelets.

Choose tools appropriate for the size eyelets you are using. A ball-peen hammer is convenient to have in your studio also.

Eyelet and setting tools

Hole punches you can use include the manual, office-type hole punch, hole punches that you strike with a hammer to make the holes, and the Cadillac of hole punches: the Japanese screw punch. With the Japanese screw punch, different size tips are used to punch different size holes in paper, fabric, and board books, not inexpensive, but well worth the investment if you will be punching lots of holes. Note: If you suffer from carpal tunnel syndrome or other hand ailments. The Japanese screw punch will make your life easier.

Fabric Paper

Fabric Paper is stiffened fabric from Michael Miller Memories that can be treated like paper. It has the feel of paper, doesn't ravel like fabric, and can be cut with decorative edge cutting tools, paper cutters, die cut machines, and hand punches. It can be put through many computer printers to print text directly onto the cloth.

Fixative

When using chalks, pastels, or eye shadow to color your page, you'll probably want to seal the powder so it doesn't smear or rub off. You can use an acrylic spray fixative from an art and craft supply store, or you can use hairspray. The latter is not archival quality.

Gesso

Gesso is an acrylic medium that can be used to seal board book pages before painting or applying adhesives. It provides a "toothy" finish to accept acrylic or oil mediums. Gesso is available in white or black, as well as a few other colors. If you want a particular color background, simply add acrylic paint to white gesso to create your own color.

Rotary Cutter, Ruler, and Self-Healing Mat

A rotary cutter looks like a very sharp pizza cutter—a circular cutting wheel attached to a handle. The cutters come in different sizes, which accommodate different sizes of cutting blades.

Rotary cutting tools

Due to the sharpness of the cutting blades, a special mat is required underneath the cutting area. These "self-healing" mats are available in a variety of sizes to suit every need. Acrylic rulers are resistant to cutting, and they will protect your hands while allowing you to make extremely straight cuts on multiple layers of paper or fabric.

Stamping Inks

Two basic types of stamping inks are available—dye ink and pigment ink. Most ink is available either in ready-to-use inkpads or in re-inkers, bottles of the same color ink for re-inking the pad. Re-inkers are great for using with brayers (rollers with which to apply ink by hand), stencils, sponges, and brushes on fabric and paper.

DYE INKS

These inks dry more quickly than pigment inks. Pigment ink, because of the slower drying time, is easier to use when embossing your image. If you are not familiar with embossing, ask for a demo at a stamp store.

PIGMENT INKS

These inks never dry on nonporous surfaces without help. Don't use pigment inks on glossy paper or vellum, unless you heat set or emboss the image. On porous (absorbent) surfaces, Prevent smearing by allowing pigment inks to dry thoroughly before touching them.

Some inks are acid-free, some are formulated for use on a wide variety of surfaces, including wood and metal, some are more colorfast than others. Read the packaging and ask questions at the store for more details on this quickly changing lineup of products.

Vellum

Vellum is a translucent paper available in a myriad of colors, textures, and weights. It can be purchased through scrapbook stores, stationary stores, and office supply stores. The lightest weight is sometimes referred to as architect's vellum, drafting vellum, or tissue vellum. C&T Publishing's Simple Foundations Translucent Vellum Paper is a nice weight to use for scrapbooks and altered books.

Writing Tools

COPIC MARKERS

COPIC Markers are one of my favorite art tools. These markers are fast-drying, nontoxic, and dye-based. They can be refilled although I've yet to have one run dry. I use them to quickly change the color of a piece of paper I'm adding to my page. I use them to highlight the edge of a book page and to color the cut or torn edges of collage papers. You can also write with these: They are wonderful for marking on a variety of surfaces. If you're having trouble writing on your book page, try using a COPIC Marker. They come in over 200 different colors, so you can buy the ones that fit your palette preference.

NEXUS PENS

Nexus Pens are my favorite fine line pens for writing text. They are lightfast, waterproof, and archival quality. They come in a variety of colors that are very versatile for journaling in your altered board books.

Painting BACKGROUNDS

Wait! Before you stammer some comment about "not being a painter," read this section. Trust me—you can paint interesting backgrounds in your altered board books. These backgrounds are very simple, easy, fast, and incredibly fun to do. You can create backgrounds that are *uniquely yours* in four steps or less. Be bold: Read on!

Painting the base color

Supplies Needed

Rubber gloves—the inexpensive disposable ones work well

Foam brush—1" or 2" wide are most versatile

Cosmetic sponge—the wedge-shaped ones are great

A newspaper, vinyl tablecloth, or old catalog to protect your work surface

A variety of acrylic paints, dye inks, calligraphy inks, and stamp pads

Decide what color you want your background to be, and gather all of the paints, inks, and stamp pads that are close to belonging in that color family. Say, for example, you want a green background for your altered board book. Get out your yellow-green stamp pad, your blue-green paint, and your olive green ink. If you don't have a wide variety of colors, it's no big deal—mix the ones you do have together in varying amounts to make a variety of tints and shades. All of the mediums mentioned can work together.

A variety of paint and ink

Tip *A clean Styrofoam egg carton makes a terrific disposable container for mixing small quantities of colors.*

Follow these steps to paint your background:

1. Use a foam brush to apply the lightest color paint or ink to your prepped board book page. Don't obsess about even or thorough paint coverage—just get some color onto most of the page. If you want to color the edges of the board book pages, feel free to do that at any time, with any of your related colors. Allow the paint or ink to dry.

2. Place a few drops of each of your related ink or paint colors onto a clean palette. I like to use between 2 and 5 related colors for this step.

Tip *Use clean lids from food containers and throw them away when you are finished.*

With a wedge-shaped cosmetic sponge, pick up a bit of each of your ink or paint colors and start dabbing them onto the colored page. Use the side of the cosmetic sponge to spread the inks all around on the page. Allow to dry.

Adding Inks

Tip *Don't have inks? Thin your acrylic paint with glazing medium to stretch the color and to make them somewhat translucent.*

3. Rub your stamp pad over the dry page. This will highlight some high and low areas of the page and give it texture. Use one stamp pad, or 2 if you have appropriate colors. Let dry.

Use a stamp pad directly on the page for lots of color or just highlights.

4. Use a tiny stamp pad or some ink on your gloved finger to highlight the edges of the page. I like to use at least one shade darker here, or try using a complementary color to add some extra "punch" to your altered board book page. Allow page to dry thoroughly, and heat set if required by any of the products you used.

See how easy and fun this is? I knew you could do it!

Easy Textured BACKGROUNDS

One of the great advantages of working in board books is that the strong pages can handle extra weight. Take advantage of the board book page stability by adding texture to the background of your altered book spreads. Here are a few easy, quick, and inexpensive ways of adding visual texture to your altered board books. These ideas should get you started thinking about *texture* as a way to enhance your finished altered book spreads. Throughout this book, you'll see other examples of these techniques used in completed book spreads.

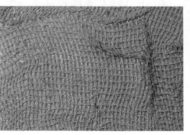

Cheesecloth creates a great texture. Spread adhesive on your board book page, then arrange your cheesecloth over the adhesive. Cover with waxed paper and use your hand to press it firmly. Allow the adhesive to dry before proceeding.

OPTION: For another layer of interest, paint your page before applying adhesive and layer painted cheesecloth on top.

Another quick, easy way to add texture is by adding some pumice gel (available at art supply stores) or clean, dry sand to paint before you apply the paint to the page.

Drywall joint tape from the hardware store is wonderful stuff! Tape it in your book, and paint over it to create a subtle grid texture.

For added visual texture, paint the board book page *before* adding drywall joint tape. Use a stamp pad or a light touch with a sponge to highlight the tape a different color than the background.

Molding paste or spackling compound mixed with paint can be applied with a plastic knife or palette knife.

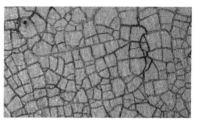

Tissue paper is a very inexpensive material for adding texture without adding weight to your altered board book. For this page, the tissue paper was painted, allowed to dry, then scrunched and glued into the book.

You can achieve a slightly different look from the same tissue paper by gluing it into your book first, and then painting the entire page.

Look at home improvement stores for discontinued rolls of textured wallpaper. Simply add paint and highlights before gluing them to the board book page for very fast, easy texture.

This crackle medium technique requires a few minutes more than the others shown, but results in a very satisfying background texture. Follow the instructions on the package of crackle medium to create this unique texture. Enhance the finished look by rubbing the dry, crackled surface with a contrasting color of paint.

Text IN ALTERED BOARD BOOKS

Whether you are creating an altered scrapbook, compiling field notes, or exploring a special topic while you are altering board books, chances are good that somewhere along the way you are going to want to incorporate *some* kind of text onto your pages. Just as there are many different ways to say what you want to say, there are many different ways to get words onto pages. Let's explore some of the easiest ways to get text into altered board books. You'll see lots more examples of text as you continue through this book.

Tip

Choose a writing tool appropriate for your background media. When writing on fabric, use a pen specially formulated for fabric so it won't smear. If writing on a slippery background, try COPIC Markers. Whatever you choose, practice on a scrap to be sure you are achieving your desired results before working directly on your actual book page.

For this altered scrapbook spread, I drew pencil lines freehand and used a metallic pencil for the journaling. If you prefer straight lines, use a straight edge.

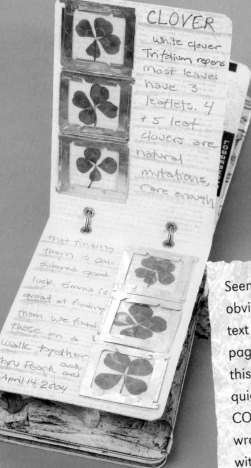

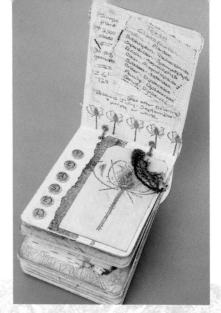

Seemingly, the most obvious way of getting text onto a board book page is by writing. For this Clover spread, I quickly drew lines with a COPIC Marker, and then wrote my *Field Notes* with pencil.

For the Carolina Wren spread in *Field Notes*, I used my computer printer to print onto tissue vellum, and glued that onto the book page after the ink was dry.

If you are nervous about writing directly on your book page, or if you want to create a layered look, write on separate pieces of paper and glue those onto your book page, as I did for this Teasel page in *Field Notes*. Teasel stamp by Fred B. Mullett.

Printing on Fragile or Thin Paper

If you have a fragile paper to which you would like to print text or images from your computer printer or copy machine, here is an easy way to accomplish that goal.

1. Print or copy your image onto regular copy paper for placement.

2. Apply double stick tape to the paper you just printed. Be especially careful to have tape at the "leading edge" of your paper and along the sides.

3. Place your fragile paper onto the double stick tape. This stabilizes the fragile paper and allows easier feeding through most printers.

4. Reprint onto this layered paper, and allow the ink to dry.

5. Carefully remove the fragile paper from the double-sided tape.

NOTE: If you need the fragile paper to be the entire size of the sheet of paper, use removable double stick tape. It will allow easier separation of your fragile paper after printing.

TIP

Prevent pencil, pastel, and chalk from smearing by finishing with a light spray of fixative, or try hairspray as a fixative.

Label makers are a very easy, inexpensive way to get text onto altered board book pages, as shown on this sea turtle page from *Field Notes*. Stamps from Turtle Press.

Taking the computer printer one step further, print your text and cut it apart before adhering it into your altered board book, as Lelainia N. Lloyd did for this spread in *Wisdom for the Journey*.

Using letters printed on your computer printer or letters cut from a magazine, you can arrange single letters to spell out what you want to say, as shown on this spread from *Field Notes*.

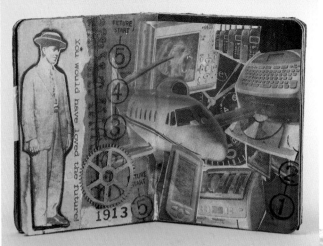

Head to your nearest scrapbook or craft store to find an incredible selection of alphabet stickers and cutouts. Julia Slebos used a wonderful, whimsical alphabet for this spread in *Julibet Lives*.

Rubber stamp alphabets are a very fun way to express yourself in your altered board books. In this spread from *Daddy*, Julia Slebos is showing her father what he would have seen if he had lived in the present.

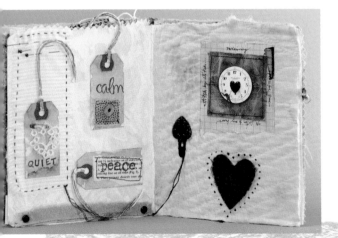

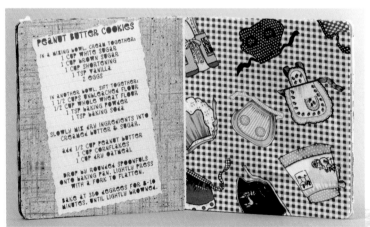

Kristin C. Steiner used a variety of rubber stamp alphabets as well as her beautiful handwriting on this page from *I Love To Sew*.

One of the simplest ways of getting text into your books is simply to print onto a loose sheet of paper and glue that onto your board book page, as shown in *My Favorite Recipes*. Fabrics by Michael Miller Fabrics.

Handwriting, letters from magazines, fragments of pages torn from books, photocopied letters, and even fabric with text on it—all combine beautifully for this spread on words in Kristin C. Steiner's altered book, *to map the treasures of my heart*.

Becky Laslie hand wrote with 3-D paint, added a vintage label, and embossed copper foil with text to complete this spread in *Curiosa*.

Another spread from *Curiosa*, by Becky Laslie, includes stamped text, wooden letters, magazine letters, and text stamped on old notebook paper.

Drying PLANT MATERIAL
IN YOUR MICROWAVE

I'll admit it: I'm an impatient person. I often decide that I want to add some type of plant material to an altered board book project, only to discover that I don't have any of that plant already dry. Out of necessity, I've figured out a way to handle this situation, using my kitchen microwave.

NOTE: Be sure to thoroughly clean your microwave after performing this task. You never know what insecticides, herbicides, or other substances may have been on that plant when it was harvested.

Follow these steps to dry plants in your microwave:

1. Harvest the plant material: leaves, stems, buds, seeds, or flowers. Use your fingers to gently flatten and arrange them.
2. Place the plant material between clean sheets of paper. This is a great place to recycle various types of paper.

NOTE: If you use paper with text on it, the ink might transfer to your plant material.

3. Layer the plant material, sandwiched in paper, between multiple layers of clean paper towels.
4. Place all of this between 2 uncoated ceramic tiles.

Tip *Look at your local hardware or home store for tiles to use for this purpose. Be sure the tile will lie flat inside your microwave.*

5. Place this entire sandwich—tile, paper towel, paper, plant material, another layer of paper, more paper towel, topped with the other ceramic tile—into your microwave.
6. Set your microwave on high for 60 seconds. Depending on the number of items you are drying and their thickness, they may need more time.

7. Allow the plant material to cool before deciding if it needs more time in the microwave. Repeat the microwave process in 20-second increments until your plant material is totally dry. Let cool completely before using in your altered board book.
8. Take notes on the total time required to dry your plant, so you'll know how much time to start with next time.
9. When placing the dried plant material in your altered book project, you have several options—matte medium, semigloss medium, or gloss medium—depending on your desired finished look.
10. You can apply the gel medium directly to the back of your plant material, carefully using a foam brush and a light touch, or you can coat the entire page with medium and then arrange the plant material on top of the page. Cover the plant material with wax paper and press completely to adhere to the book page.

NOTE: All microwaves perform at different rates. Be sure to check your plant material frequently, and be careful when removing the tiles from the microwave—they might be hot!

Dried plant materials are used in altered board Books. Kudzu and Leaves are (at right) from *Field Notes*. Flowers are (above) from Joyce M.A. Gary's *Nature* altered book.

CREATING A Niche

Sometimes you may want to put something big in your altered board book. Well, maybe not really big, but thicker than your board book pages. This is the perfect time to make a niche. A niche is simply a cutout, or recessed area. With a sharp cutting tool and a little patience, you can create a simple niche quite easily.

Follow these steps to create a niche in your altered board book:

1. Plan how large and deep you want your niche to be, based on the item(s) you want to put in them. Lightly pencil the cutting lines on the top board book page of the niche.

2. Place a cutting mat underneath the last page you intend to cut, making sure you have at least one board book page left intact behind your niche to serve as the back of your cutout.

3. Using a straight edge and a sharp cutting tool, carefully score along each cut edge.

4. It's better to make multiple, light-pressure passes with the blade instead of one pass using lots of pressure.

5. After you've finished cutting the niche, you have a choice: You may apply adhesive around the outer edges of the boards, as well as around the inner newly cut edges, or you may leave the cut boards unglued and work the niche into the overall design of each of your pages.

6. Decorate with paint or paper as you wish, and attach your items inside your niche.

Delores Hamilton used simple cutouts to create a frame on every spread in *Garden Sonnets*.

Joyce M.A. Gary created this niche in *Nature* to hold real specimens. Notice the wonderful painted and stamped background, as well as the stencil letters from Ma Vinci's Reliquary.

Becky Laslie created this deep niche in *Curiosa* and framed the cut edges with copper foil. Notice the wonderful handwritten text on the left side of this spread.

Setting EYELETS

Eyelets are wonderful things. They can add a finishing visual touch to your work, or they can serve as the reinforcement for holding your altered board book pages together. Available in many shapes, colors, and sizes, they can be whimsical, functional, or both. For altered board books, look for long eyelets from the scrapbook or craft store, or use larger, two-part eyelets from the fabric store.

Supplies Needed
Eyelets
Eyelet setting tool
Hole punch—in a size appropriate for your eyelets
Mat board, acrylic board, or scrap wood to protect your work surface
Hammer

How to Set an Eyelet
Be sure you pay attention to the size of the eyelet *before* punching the hole. Too small of a hole can be remedied; too large of a hole will not hold your eyelet in place.

The hole punch could be a manual one, like you might remember from grade school; a "hit-with-a-hammer" hole punch available from scrapbook stores; or the Cadillac of hole punches, the Japanese screw punch. See the Glossary of Materials on page 8 and Online Resources on page 47 for more information on these tools.

Now that you have checked to be sure you have the appropriate size hole punch for your eyelet, follow these steps to set an eyelet:

1. Punch the hole through all the layers you want to include in the eyelet. Place the eyelet in the hole.

Punching holes for eyelet

2. Place the eyelet through the punched hole.

Eyelet in place

3. Turn the eyelet and book page over and place it on a firm surface.

Tip *An acrylic cutting board is a terrific surface to use when setting eyelets. Acrylic boards can be purchased inexpensively or recycled from your kitchen, so there's no need to worry about making marks on it.*

4. If you are using a 2-part eyelet, place the other part of the washer in place.
5. Take your eyelet setting tool and a small- to medium-size hammer. Firmly tap the hammer onto the eyelet setting tool 2–3 times. Remove the tool from the eyelet and check to see if the edges are flaring. It is the flaring out of the back of the eyelet that holds the layers together, and holds the second part of the eyelet (if you are using one).

Setting the eyelet

Congratulations! You have successfully set your eyelet. Remember, practice does improve your skills, so if you are not thrilled with how your eyelet looks, try again. Practice will help you determine how many taps with the hammer you need to use and how much of your arm strength you need to apply with each tap in order to be happy with your outcome.

Paper BACKGROUNDS

One of the easiest ways to achieve interesting backgrounds in altered board books is to use readily available scrapbook papers. There is seemingly no end to the variety of papers available at your local scrapbook or craft store. From rustic-looking papers like those from the Paper Loft to vintage-inspired papers from 7gypsies, to soft papers from Colorbök, treat yourself to a trip to the nearest scrapbook store to see a wide selection! (For web addresses of these companies, see Online Resources on page 47.)

When adhering paper to a board book page, you have three methods to choose from. I've found the following methods easiest. These recommendations are based on my experience altering board books.

TIP *For each of these methods, I recommend cutting your background papers slightly larger than the desired finished size, then trimming the edges after adhering the paper into the book. It is difficult to place a perfectly cut piece of paper exactly straight on the board book base, so starting larger and trimming makes the process much easier. If you have a favorite paper adhesive, use it.*

OPTION 1. Use a Xyron machine to apply dry adhesive to the back of your decorative paper. Peel away the protective sheet, then carefully place your paper onto the board book page, aligning the center edge with the center of the book. It can be very difficult to reposition Xyron-backed paper, so use great care when positioning your paper. Use the edge of the board book page as a cutting guide to trim away the excess paper with a rotary cutter or X-Acto knife.

OPTION 2. Use a good-quality glue stick to completely coat the board book page. Place your paper in the book, aligning the center edge with the center of the book. Press with the heel of your hand to ensure a good connection. After the glue is dry, use the edge of the board book page as a cutting guide to trim away the excess paper with a rotary cutter or X-Acto knife.

OPTION 3. Using liquid or white paper glue, follow the same procedure as in option 2, substituting the liquid adhesive for the glue stick. Use a paintbrush or a plastic key card to spread your adhesive on the board book pages. After the glue is dry, use the edge of the board book page as a cutting guide to trim away the excess paper with a rotary cutter or X-Acto knife.

After the background paper is in place, you are ready to proceed. Add collage elements, photographs, text, metal objects—whatever you want to use to complete each spread.

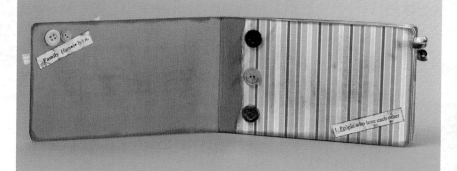

Friend (frend), 1. One who entertains for another such sentiments of esteem, respect, and affection that he seeks his society and welfare; a well-wisher; an intimate associate. 2. Person who favours and supports. 3. Person who belongs to the same side or group.

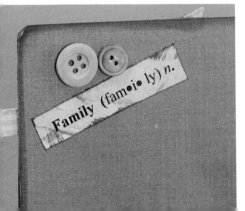

Family (fam•i•ly) n.

One of the easiest and most rewarding ways of getting started in book art is to create a scrapbook or gift book for yourself or someone you care about. Lelainia N. Lloyd created simple paper collage bases ready for the recipient to add photos, honor friendships, and record dreams for their future.

Altered board book pages do not have to be complicated to be successful. Fabric, office supply store hardware, stamps, stitching, an old report card, and color copies of textbook covers combine to make simple nostalgic spreads in this oversized altered board book. Note the use of 2-part eyelets used to hold these pages together. Paper from The Paper Loft.

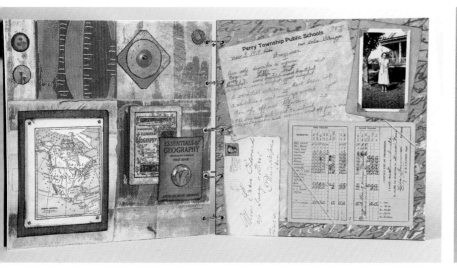

Paper makes great background material for altered accordion board books, too. In her *Field Notes*, Lelainia N. Lloyd used rustic scrapbook paper enhanced with Ranger Distress inks as a basis for nature stamping and collected ephemera.

This spread from my *Italy* book uses another wonderful Paper Loft paper background. Stamped architecture, combined with parts of a collage sheet from Rubber Baby Buggy Bumpers, makes a simple old-world spread.

Collections from a trip to Myrtle Beach were simply glued onto this background in *Field Notes*.

This Pansy drawing was done on the same vellum used for the background, then torn to fit the book page.

For *Field Notes*, I layered 2 different papers for the background of each page. The first layer is a page from an old U.S. Department of Agriculture *Yearbook* that I painted with a light coat of gesso and beige paint to make the text less visible. The top layer is scrunched vellum attached to the page and then trimmed to fit.

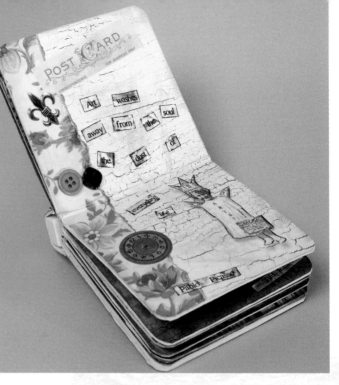

Altered board books don't require a serious theme, nor do you have to have a large collection of ephemera to have fun. This *Girlfriends* book was made with Colorbök papers and 3-D sticker sets. What a fun, simple project to make for a special girl. Stickers make this project easy enough for a child to make. Consider adding photographs of the girl's best friends or providing gel pens for writing messages.

Wisdom for the Journey, made by Lelainia N. Lloyd, is built on wonderful background papers. The collage elements support the quote on each precious spread.

For her book *HAIR art,* Delores Hamilton used the same face rubber stamp from Stamp Francisco and graphic background paper for each altered board book page. She created unique hair art for each woman by using a variety of materials: stamped artwork, found objects, and feathers.

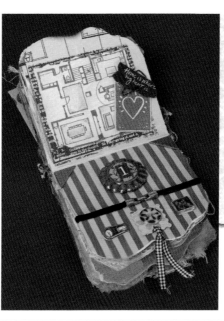

Kristin C. Steiner used tissue paper, scrapbook paper, and a copy of an old gardening book as the background to these gardening and architecture spreads in her altered board book, *to map the treasures of my heart.*

Delores Hamilton used paper exclusively to create the landscapes in her altered board book *This Land Is My Land.*

Carol Owen created her altered board book *Three Sisters Star Book* by using multiple layers of paper when she collaged each wonderful spread. Vintage papers, stamps, strategically placed pockets, flaps, and metal embellishments all come together in this incredible book.

Fabric BACKGROUNDS

Fabrics make wonderful backgrounds in altered board books. From quilting cottons, to sheer gauze, to luscious silks, indulge in some tactile textiles for your next altered book project. Simple to use and readily available, cloth is something everyone has a history with—after all it's been next to our skin from the time we were born.

Fabrics often require slightly different treatment than papers. The following is a description of the easiest way of getting fabric onto your altered board book pages.

How to Adhere Fabric to Altered Board Book Page

1. When using fabric for a full-page background, I recommend cutting the fabric slightly larger than the desired finished size and trimming it after it is adhered to your book page. Be sure to have at least one straight edge.

2. Spread adhesive on the prepped board.

> **Tip** *Use an old hotel key card or expired phone card to spread a thin layer of adhesive.*

> **Tip** *Even when you need a straight cut, you can still use a decorative edge rotary cutter to make it. This is especially useful when you have a fabric that frays easily.*

3. Carefully place your fabric or fabric-paper onto the adhesive, placing the straight edge at the center fold at the spine of the book. When you are satisfied with placement, smooth the fabric or fabric-paper into place, using your hand to ensure good contact all over the page.

4. Repeat on the opposite side of the spread.

5. Place a piece of waxed paper between the pages, close the book, and place it under a heavy book or other weight to dry. This will reduce warping of your pages and ensure a professional-looking finished product.

6. After the adhesive is dry, use your rotary cutter or X-Acto knife to carefully trim the excess fabric from around the edges of the pages.

> **Tip** *For fabrics that unravel easily is to cut them slightly off-grain to reduce the amount of fraying.*

My Favorite Recipes is an altered cookbook that is great for a quick, personalized gift. This book would be perfect for a wedding shower or for someone in his or her first apartment. Consider making one for a unique housewarming gift. Collect family recipes to share with your child, or make an altered cookbook using the recipient's favorite foods: the dishes you know they need to have to be happy. Perhaps there is a gourmet cook on your gift list. How about collecting as many variations on a dish as you can find and letting them experiment. Use some fun fonts on your computer printer to print your recipes, or handwrite them on recipe cards. Fabric and Fabric Paper from Michael Miller Fabrics.

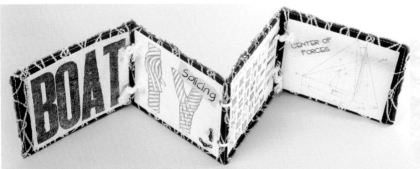

An accordion board book, covered with nautical theme fabrics may be the perfect gift for the boat lover in your family. Cut or tear fabric to size, layer decorated canvas, and then attach embellishments from the marine store. Sew around the edges, or glue the boards to the fabric, add eyelets (grommets in boat language), and tie with rope to finish the project. Be inspired by theme fabrics to make a similar book for a fly fisherman, or to remember a special cruise. Fabric from Timeless Treasures.

OTHER IDEAS: If you get seasick just thinking about the water, don't run for the nearest lifeboat: Instead, use this format to make a book focusing on a favorite sport, or use the accordion format for your own nature guide. If you prefer the indoor arena, the accordion book would be an excellent choice for any theme: yoga poses, favorite coffees or teas, favorite TV series, or your children's artwork. Or make an accordion scrapbook to give as a gift or to display on your mantle.

In *I Love to Sew*, Kristin C. Steiner combined soft fabric backgrounds with vintage sewing items to create this spread.

If you are lucky enough to have some treasured quilt fragments hidden away, consider including them in an altered book where they can be shared and enjoyed by friends and family. Kristin C. Steiner combined small patchwork blocks with vintage buttons, pattern instructions, fabric backgrounds, and words written on cotton tape to complete this joyful spread.

Tip *I love the soft edges that often result from tearing fabric. If you want to try this, tear your fabric the desired finished size before applying it to your book page because it is impractical to tear the fabric after it's in your book.*

In this spread from *Italy*, the village fabric needed no embellishment or layering. Notice the soft torn edges on this simple page accented with stamps from Stampers Anonymous and Above the Mark.

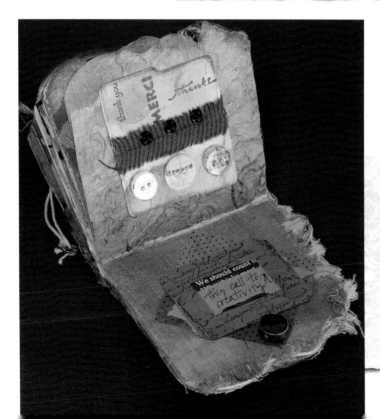

For this call to creativity spread in *to map the treasures of my heart*, Kristin C. Steiner combined torn and raveled fabric with fibers, notions, overdyed fabrics, stamping, and much more.

PAINTED BACKGROUNDS *gallery*

As you saw in the Techniques section, painting backgrounds can be fun and is very easy. What a great, personal way to achieve unique backgrounds in your altered board book. You can stick with one color family, or use complementary colors when choosing your background palette. Here are some terrific painted backgrounds to inspire you to create a unique spread in your next altered board book project.

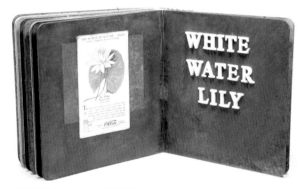

For these pages in *Wildflowers*, acrylic paint, dye ink, and chalk ink were combined to create distinctive backgrounds to complement the flower featured on each spread.

In *USA*, Lelainia N. Lloyd used acrylic paints on a dry brush over gesso prepped boards to create a soft background for her patriotic collages.

For this page in *Field Notes*, I used dye inks to simulate the safe feeling of Snug Harbor.

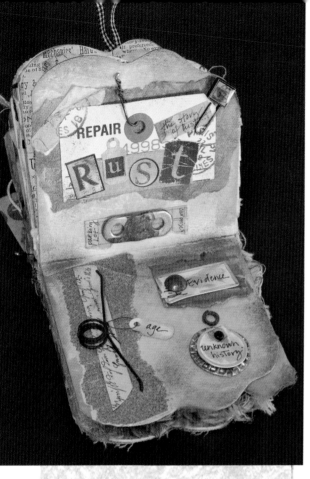

Julia Slebos honors her father in this wonderful spread in *Daddy*. A painted background supports simple collage elements, including a photograph of her father taken in 1917.

to map the treasures of my heart includes some wonderful painted backgrounds. Kristin C. Steiner used fabric, paper, metal, and wonderful embellishments to illustrate her love of muted palettes and metal objects on these two spreads from this tiny altered treasure.

In *Julibet Lives*, Julia Slebos made this humorous spread based on a photo taken of her as a young girl. The wonderful painted background sets off the toothpick leg figures.

MIXED BACKGROUNDS

Now that you've had an opportunity to try your hand at altered board books using paper, paint, and fabric backgrounds, you might be interested in combining these skills in your next project. Not all backgrounds need to be just one technique. Try, for example, combining painting and stamping, stamping on top of a paper background, or mixing fabric and paper in your next altered board book spread. There is no limit to the combinations possible. Let's see some ideas that have been successful for other people.

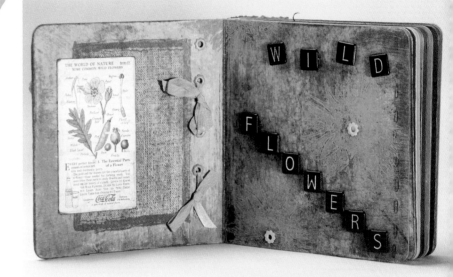

This spread in *Wildflowers* includes paint, inks, stamping, and vintage lace.

The title page inside *Wildflowers* includes a stamped, painted background. Stamps from Just For Fun, Rubber Baby Buggy Bumpers, and Stampington.

For this 1897 spread in *Daddy*, Julia Slebos included collage papers, paint, paste paper, stamping, and more.

Joyce M.A. Gary experimented with backgrounds throughout her *Journey* book. This spread includes paint, cheesecloth, and textured wallpaper.

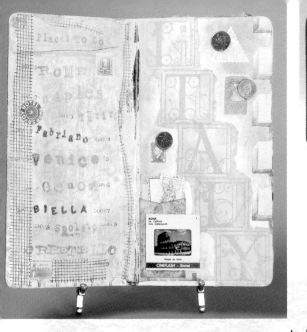

Iris and Buttercup from *Wildflowers* both have painted backgrounds stamped with hand carved stamps for additional subtle interest. The Iris letters from MaVinci's Reliquary were painted with acrylic paints. The watercolor stickers on Buttercup are from Colorbök.

This title page in *Italy* includes a sanded background, paint, ink, and stamping. Stamps by: Just For Fun, MaVinci's Reliquary, and Stampers Anonymous.

For the mermaid spread in *Alter Egos*, Joyce M.A. Gary made a paint, stencil, and collage background fit for her underwater beauty.

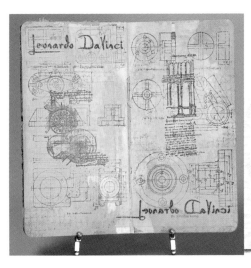

For the DaVinci spread in *Italy*, I included a peeled and sanded background, inks, paints, stamps, and ink jet transfers under the vellum images.

For the Wing Shop spread in *Alter Egos*, Joyce M.A. Gary layered a painted background with lots of stamping and stenciling before she collaged her winged beauty.

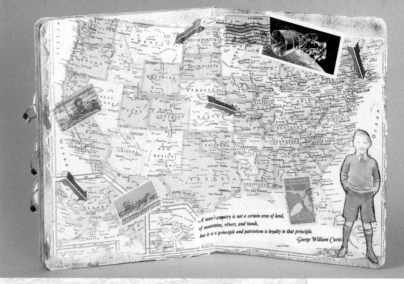

Lelainia N. Lloyd gesso and painted her altered board book pages before layering a map on which to build her collage in *USA*.

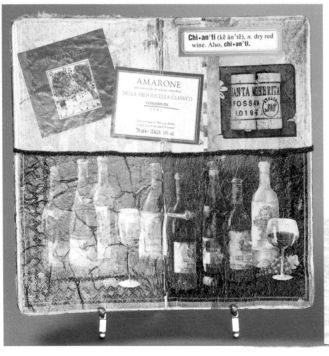

The background for Jack-in-the-Pulpit in *Wildflowers* was painted, then layered with torn and stitched handmade paper.

The Chianti spread in *Italy* includes a peeled and sanded background layered with the decorative top ply of a cocktail napkin and wine bottle labels.

In *I Love To Sew*, Kristin C. Steiner recalls the challenge of learning how to sew zippers. This spread reminds her of all the alternative closures available. Fabric and paper combine for the background of this fun page.

For the Lily spread in *Wildflowers*, I combined paint, stamping, and paper. Alphabet stamps: Mardi Gras from MaVinci's Reliquary.

It is good
to have an end
to journey
towards;
but it is
the journey
that matters
in the end.

Joyce M.A. Gary included paint, cheesecloth and alcohol based inks on these backgrounds in *Journey*. The phrase is from a stamp by Stampers Anonymous, the globe by Stamp Francisco.

Julia Slebos combined paint, stamping, and handmade paste paper to back the Man of the House in her altered board book, *Daddy*.

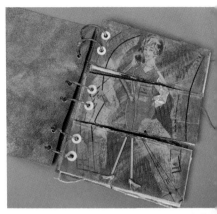

Julia Slebo's wonderful spread in *Julibet Lives* is backed by paint, Portfolio pastels, commercial and hand-carved stamps.

The background for Dutchman's Breeches in *Wildflowers* is a combination of painting and stamping. Stamp by Stampington.

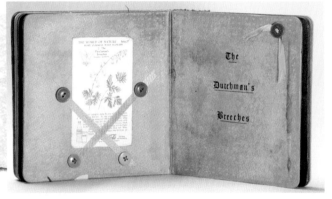

This leaf spread in Joyce M.A. Gary's altered book *Nature* has a background of paint, stamping, and real leaves.

For *Exquisite Corpse*, Becky Laslie combined fluid acrylics, pattern tissue, paint, drywall tape, transfers, and more. The book pages are divided into three equal sections so the viewer can rearrange them in different combinations.

For the Circle of Friends spread in *I Love to Sew*, Kristin C. Steiner included fabric, vintage paper, an old postcard, lace, and much more.

Vintage Girl, a spread in *to map the treasures of my heart* by Kristin C. Steiner, includes fabric, paper, lace, and functional hinges.

Squirrel Dreams in *Field Notes* includes scrunched vellum, stamping (Stampers Anonymous, Rubber Baby Buggy Bumper), vintage notebook paper, and ink.

This spread from *Curiosa* by Becky Laslie includes paint, gel transfers, metal, stamping, stitching, painted drywall tape, and more.

COVER ART *gallery*

As you begin or continue to work in altered board books, you'll see that there is no formula for a successful cover for your project. Some covers will come very easily for you, and others may be more challenging. Sometimes you'll get the perfect idea for the cover while you are working inside the book, and other times the cover will be the last thing you do when completing your altered book. Just recognizing that "not all covers are created equally" will help you relax and realize that eventually you'll come up with the ideal cover for your project.

One reason that I enjoy cover art is that it allows you to do even more dimensional work than the spreads inside an altered board book. You don't have to concern yourself with what is going to be in front of the cover, so there is no limit on materials. The following examples are intended to inspire you to have fun with your altered board book covers.

The cover of *Girlfriends* gets its fun, simple look from Colorbök scrapbook papers and 3-D stickers. A simple square cutout reveals the best friends inside.

After applying gesso and dry brushing acrylic paint onto the cover of *USA*, Lelainia N. Lloyd added scrapbook paper and collage items to create this patriotic cover.

ME, an altered board book made by Lelainia N. Lloyd, is a gift scrapbook with lots of room inside for the recipient to add photos and mementoes. She used reversible scrapbook papers and downloaded fonts to create this retro-inspired cover.

This front cover from *School Days* relies on the wonderful rustic papers from the Paper Loft, combined with sticker letters from Colorbök. The cover is simple, quick, and effective.

Joyce M.A. Gary took advantage of the extra-dimensional opportunities when she created this cover for *Journey*. She combined corrugated cardboard, metal, and stamping for this simple cover collage.

Using decorated papers for the silhouettes and letters by Wordsworth, Joyce M.A. Gary created this wonderful cover for her altered board book *Alter Egos*.

The cover of *I Love to Sew* by Kristin C. Steiner uses fabric and buttons to entice the viewer to pick it up and look inside.

The cover of *HAIR art* by Delores Hamilton gives a preview of the fun inside.

For the cover of *My Favorite Recipes*, I added another small, fabric altered board book onto the cover of the cookbook. This tiny book includes information on measuring and common abbreviations used in cookbooks. Use a strong adhesive to attach the board books. The vintage kitchen fabrics are from Michael Miller Fabrics.

For the cover of my son's *Lego* altered scrapbook, we built the letters from real Lego pieces.

Kristin C. Steiner used fabric, mica, text, walnut ink, and more to create the cover of *to map the treasures of my heart*. She used shoe polish to enhance textured wallpaper and stamped on cotton tape to create a safe haven for the book when traveling.

A fiber-wrapped handle, some scrapbook paper, and vintage images combine with a simple title on the cover of Lelainia N. Lloyd's altered board book *Wisdom for the Journey*.

For the cover of *Field Notes*, I combined paper, birch bark, hammered metal, and a found critter tail.

Julia Slebos altered photos of herself as a little girl for the cover of *Julibet Lives!*

Taking advantage of the additional opportunities of cover space, I painted distressed silk flower parts and stitched leaves to the painted front of *Wildflowers*. Note the color-enhanced suede fabric strip glued on to reinforce the binding area of the book.

For the cover of *Daddy*, Julia Slebos rubbed shoe polish over masking tape and layered stamped metal and her father's photograph in a vintage microscope slide mailer.

On this cover of *Curiosa*, Becky Laslie painted, collaged found objects, and wired a twig to the binding edge for a finishing touch.

CONTRIBUTING ARTISTS

Joyce Gary
Atlanta, Georgia

Delores Hamilton
Cary, North Carolina

Becky Laslie
Brighton, Michigan
**www.alteredbookartists.com/gallery/
memberspages/laslie.html**

Lelainia N. Lloyd
Coquitlam, British Columbia
http://members.shaw.ca/tatterededge

Carol Owen
Pittsboro, North Carolina
www.carolowenart.com

Julia Slebos
Durham, North Carolina

Jan Bode Smiley
Fort Mill, South Carolina
www.jansmiley.com

Kristin C. Steiner
Columbia, South Carolina
kbsteiner@surfbest.net

ON-LINE RESOURCES

**FOR MORE INFORMATION ON
ALTERED BOOKS:**
International Society of Altered
Book Artists
**www.alteredbookartists.com/index.
html**

Altered Book Group
**www.groups.yahoo.com/group/altered
books**

OTHER ON-LINE RESOURCES:
Copyright Information For
Collage Artists
www.funnystrange.com/copyright

FABRICS:
Cotton and linen fabrics prepared
to print on ink jet printers
www.Colortextiles.com

Michael Miller Fabrics—Great retro
fabrics, Fabric Paper
www.michaelmillerfabrics.com

Timeless Treasures fabrics
www.ttfabrics.com

**PAPER AND OTHER
SCRAPBOOK/ALTERED BOOK
SUPPLIES:**
Colorbŏk – scrapbook paper, 3-D
and metal embellishments
www.colorbok.com

The Paper Loft LLC – incredible papers
and alphabet stickers
www.paperloft.com

7 gypsies – printed twill tape, interesting
papers, journal hardware, lots more
www.7gypsies.com/

RUBBER STAMPS:
Fred Mullett Rubber Stamps
 www.fredbmullett.com

Hot Potatoes
www.hotpotatoes.com

Jessie's alphabet and other great
rubber stamp alphabets:
www.turtlearts.com

Just For Fun Rubber Stamps
www.jffstamps.com

MaVinci's Reliquary – incredible variety
of rubber stamp alphabets
http://crafts.dm.net/mall/reliquary

Stampers Anonymous
www.stampersanonymous.com

Stampington & Company
www.stampington.com

OTHER RECOMMENDED PRODUCTS:
Blank Board Books and Color Tool,
Carol Doak's Foundation Paper, and
Simple Foundations Translucent
 Vellum Paper
www.ctpub.com

Golden Paints and Mediums
www.goldenpaints.com

Jo Sonya's Paints
www.josonjas.com

Junkitz - Self adhesive zippers,
buttons, zipper pulls
www.junkitz.com

Ranger Distress Ink & Archival Ink
www.rangerink.com

Copic Markers
www.copicmarker.com/

Nexus Pens
www.chartpak.com/index2.html

ABOUT THE AUTHOR

Jan Smiley is an author and mixed media artist. She began her artistic life as a quilt maker, and took those skills with her as she crossed over into book arts, where she takes great pleasure in merging the mediums.

First carving her own stamps for use on paper and fabric, then learning about altered books, visual journals, and scrapbooks, she enjoys exploring the unlimited potential of combining her interests.

INDEX